simple life lessons

by lindsay sealey

© Copyright 2002 Lindsay Sealey. All rights reserved.

No part of this publication may be reproduced, stored in a retrieval system, or transmitted, in any form or by any means, electronic, mechanical, photocopying, recording, or otherwise, without the written prior permission of the author.

Printed in Victoria, Canada

```
National Library of Canada Cataloguing in Publication

Sealey, Lindsay, 1976-
    Simple life lessons, or, Simple treasures /
Lindsay Sealey.

ISBN 1-55395-117-4
    I. Title.   II. Title: Simple treasures.
BF637.S4S423 2002        158.1     C2002-904572-X
```

TRAFFORD

This book was published *on-demand* in cooperation with Trafford Publishing.
On-demand publishing is a unique process and service of making a book available for retail sale to the public taking advantage of on-demand manufacturing and Internet marketing. **On-demand publishing** includes promotions, retail sales, manufacturing, order fulfilment, accounting and collecting royalties on behalf of the author.

Suite 6E, 2333 Government St., Victoria, B.C. V8T 4P4, CANADA

Phone	250-383-6864	Toll-free	1-888-232-4444 (Canada & US)
Fax	250-383-6804	E-mail	sales@trafford.com
Web site	www.trafford.com		TRAFFORD PUBLISHING IS A DIVISION OF TRAFFORD HOLDINGS LTD.
Trafford Catalogue #02-0831		www.trafford.com/robots/02-0831.html	

10   9   8   7   6   5   4   3

Contents

Introduction	iv
Acknowledgements	vii
Dedication	x
Joy	1
Smiling	3
Balance	5
Timing	8
Learning	10
Focus	13
Success	16
People	19
Dreaming	23
Community	26
Diversity	29
Self-acceptance	32
Thoughts	35
Opportunity	38
Disappointment	41
Passion	44

Contents

Happiness	47
Fear	50
Growth	53
Attitude	55
Goals	58
Self-discovery	61
Self-care	63
Encouragement	66
Discipline	69
Boundaries	71
Peace	74
Proactivity	77
Clarity	80
Emotions	83
Surrender	86
Healing	89
Vulnerability	92

Contents

Timing	96
Celebration	99
Denial	102
Perspective	106
Boredom	110
Perfection	112
Patience	115
Prayer	118
Friendship	121
Gratitude	125
Generosity	128
Reflecting	132
Pain	136
Purpose	139
About the Author	142

Introduction

I have always been an avid reader of self-help books. I thoroughly enjoy learning about other people's experiences and relishing their insights in order to learn more about myself. I feel I am on a continual quest for knowledge and understanding. I also feel the better able we are to understand ourselves and our purpose in this world, the more equipped we are to handle stress, take on new challenges, and help those around us.

When I started reading these kinds of books, I began to notice how much I was learning and how easily I was able to apply the teachings to my own circle of influence. Additionally, I began noticing these books were written by "mature" individuals with much life experience. I wondered if perhaps I, a less mature but highly motivated and ambitious individual, could offer both the older and younger generations an unique perspective on the world.

After my revelation I soon became filled with self-doubt and cynicism. Who was I to offer any advice? What did I really know? Who will care what I have to say? Yet, I corrected these negative, debilitating thoughts almost immediately because I knew deep down inside that I had something special to contribute. I knew that I had invaluable experiences. And I knew it was time to share my thoughts and feelings.

This book represents many things to me; a challenge I want to embrace, a dream I want to fulfill, a gift I want to give, and a time of learning I want to enjoy. I wanted to combine my love for quotations with personal experiences and insights. Reading and writing bring me great joy and I wanted to use these skills to reflect upon my life thus far. This book is a time for me to offer what I know to be true and a time to learn of what I am uncertain. I had a yearning to expand on some "simple life lessons". I really do believe that life is simple and that by becoming more aware of these imperative yet simple lessons and taking them to heart, we will all be kinder people, better equipped to help others. I hope you enjoy the never-ending journey of self-discovery as much as I have.

Acknowledgments

Any project that is taken on does not become a success without the assistance of people and hard work, dedication, and support. Therefore, I feel it is not only a privilege but also a necessity for me to say thank you to all of those who have been eternal sources of energy and encouragement.

First and foremost I want to thank God for providing me with a diversity of experiences from which I have been able to learn and grow. Thank you for teaching me the enormity of Your love and strength. To my dad, whose support, care, kindness, and charisma have led me to develop in ways I never thought I could. Thank you for having such a renewed zest for life and for always being there for me. To my brother, Lawson, I hope you know how much I appreciate having your solidity to lean on. You are such a pillar of strength, and I envy and admire your balanced perspective on life.

To all my friends, I truly and genuinely appreciate each and every one of you for being such special and unique people, for always helping me feel good about myself, and for believing I could do it. I love you all with all my heart. To the VOC Choir, such a blessing and a privilege to be surrounded by such loving and talented people. I am so grateful to be a part of the choir; to have the opportunity to reach out to others and to share love and hope. Thanks to Checo for demonstrating such love and compassion and for "keeping it real". Thank you to my classmates and colleagues who remind me daily the importance of balance, perspective, principles, and purpose. I have learned a tremendous amount from all of you about learning, leadership, and life.

Finally, to all the readers who can learn from my thoughts and insights: I truly hope I can make a difference in your lives and help in the actualizing of great potential!

Dedication

I would like to dedicate this book to all of those who have loved me unconditionally and blessed me with the opportunity and freedom to grow, develop, and become the person I am meant to be. I am eternally grateful for the inspiration, encouragement, and wisdom that I have been blessed with along my journey.

Joy

"Joy is not in things; it is in us."
- Richard Wagner

I believe that joy is within each of us. I also believe that not everybody knows or believes this to be true. For me, joy is manifested in many things: the laughter of children, a warm and loving smile, or a magnificent sunset. Moreover, joy is the energy and enthusiasm within me that helps me to feel completely content and at peace with life. Joy is not a place or a tangible thing but, rather, a knowing that everything is all right. Joy emerges when we take time to do the things that demand our attention, when we make time to listen and share with people, when we can enjoy each moment of each day, and when we can give to people and know we make a difference in their lives. The very nature of joy is a celebration of love and gratitude. We all have joy. We just have to release it from within.

True joy comes from living in the moment and appreciating the uniqueness of each and every day.

Smiling

"A smile is worth a thousand words."
- Unknown

Smiling is my gift to others. I love to smile at people and convey my inner joy and happiness. I feel that smiling is a reflection of how I am feeling, and it is by smiling that I share my contentment. I may not have a lot to offer, and I may not have a lot of time with the abundance of people I come into contact with on a daily basis. However, one thing I do have is a smile. Smiling is my opportunity to make a connection with another human being and perhaps give some hope. Smiling can be bonding, healing, comforting, encouraging, joyful, and hopeful. A smile can literally say it all.

When I smile, I give and, in turn, receive. Even if a person doesn't return my smile, I am convinced it impacts them. Those who are down may feel uplifted. Those who are distraught may feel comforted. Those without hope may feel illuminated.

A smile is a simple act of kindness. It doesn't cost money. It barely takes any effort at all. But the effects of a smile can make all the difference in the world.

Balance

"We can train ourselves to become more yielding, balanced, and flexible, giving up our rigid stance, and fixed ideas."
- Lama Surya Das

I'll be the first to admit that I live a life of imbalance. More often than not, I put work and school before people and activities. Once I get into "work mode" I find it extremely difficult to take a break from this momentum and have some fun. What does balance mean? Balanced living is the ability to devote time to all areas of life: social, emotional, physical, mental, familial, and spiritual so that we can attain personal well-being, peace of mind, and harmony with ourselves.

Balanced living requires effort. I know that I am not alone in my "workaholic" tendencies. Many people share my "need" to be committed to my vocation. Maybe your imbalance does not manifest in your work. Perhaps you overeat, overexercize, or overspend. Whether you devote your time to socializing, studying, or exercising, the key is moderation. I know that I must make a conscious effort to fulfill all areas of my life. This requires me to write down commitments and fill in a "balance wheel" so that I do what I say I will do. Tedious as this may sound, the result is a happier, healthier, individual who is aware of times of both balance and imbalance and who can act accordingly to maintain a sense of equilibrium.

There are definitely times when we need to be more devoted to certain tasks or people than we may be at other times. This is life. But the point is that continual assessment is essential in order to living in balance.

Balanced living requires time and effort but the result is a healthy, happy individual with a better understanding of moderation.

Timing

"If we could untangle the mysteries of life and unravel the energies which run through the world; if we could evaluate correctly the significance of passing events; if we could measure the struggles, dilemmas, and aspirations of mankind, we could find that nothing is born out of time. Everything comes at its appointed moment."
- Joseph R. Sizoo

Time is a constant. It goes on regardless of circumstance. Time is really a life force in and of itself. Yet even with this knowledge we feel a need to change time in accordance with our own schedules. We may find we are always dissatisfied with time. When we are having fun and content with the moment, we want time to stand still.

When we are deep in sorrow and feeling as though life has the best of us, we can't wait for time to pass. Speed up, slow down, or stand still time will not. Time really does act independently of us.

    Timing is everything. There is both a time and a season for every life event. Everything happens for a reason. Timing, even if we may not believe it, is perfect. Wait until the time is right. Both acting too soon and acting too late are self-defeating behaviors. Both are ineffective. When the time is right, and you will know when it is, act - and do what needs to be done.

Be patient, keeping in mind that everything happens at the exact moment it is meant to happen.

Learning

"Life is a Gentle Teacher. She wants to help us learn. The lessons she wants to teach us are the ones we need to learn...She will keep repeating the lesson until we learn it."
- Melody Beattie

Life is an endless opportunity to learn. As a lifelong learner, I have always been inspired and motivated to learn and, in turn, educate. I feel I have an open, imaginative, ever-expanding mind. And I pride myself on my ability to build on my knowledge on a daily basis. Whether I am learning about academic subjects, relationships, or myself, I know I am constantly growing and progressing.

The ability to learn and the quest for knowledge is a gift, and one I treasure dearly. Learning helps me feel confident and high in esteem. Thinking about the ways of the world and human behavior ensure I am always rising to a higher level of understanding.

Learning can be overwhelming and exhilarating at times. There is so much to learn. We can become easily frustrated and want to give up. But learning is not a destination; it is a process. There is no time limit. There is no hurry. Learning is an ever-available journey and a journey we are meant to enjoy.

Life is an exciting progression of lessons.

Focus

"When you stay focused and keep commitment you create momentum, and momentum creates momentum".
- Rich Fettke

I have always been extremely focused. It is almost as if I was born with a vision. Not only do I see the vision, but I am able to take the necessary steps to reach that vision. I keep on track by being organized, planning, doing the work, being disciplined, managing my time effectively and then reflecting on my actions so that I can see what is working and what needs improving.

Being focused is devoting time and attention to what matters, living a life with purpose, being on target, and doing what is best for you. By having clear direction, I feel I am able to reach my goals and achieve much success. Being focused allows me to feel very prosperous; I always feel very proud of who I am and high in esteem when I do what I say I am going to do and when I see the results of my hard work and dedication.

I choose to focus my energy on the positive aspects of my life. I am focused on school, work, friends, family, and God. I choose not spend too much time on my failures, problems, miscommunications, missed opportunities, and negative people who enter my life. It is easy to shift one's focus and dwell on things or people that drain your energy. However, by being aware and understanding the advantages of being focused, you will learn to be focused and stay on track.

Focus your time and energy on things that are important to you: focus your thoughts, your words, and your actions and see the results!

Success

"Apparent failure may hold in its rough shell the germs of success that will blossom in time, and bear fruit throughout eternity."
- Francis Ellen Watkins Harper

Success feels fantastic. There is no doubt about it. Nothing can compare to that feeling of euphoria that accompanies reaching your goal, receiving praise, doing what you have always wanted to do, getting that raise at work, winning the prize, or making amends with a friend. Whatever you define success to be, whatever success means in your world, it is great when you can experience success and, more importantly, when you can acknowledge your feelings about your achievement.

This weekend past was a successful one for me on many levels. First, I accomplished everything I set out to do. Second, I was approached by a guy and asked out on a date (this always boosts one's ego). Third, I faced and overcame a fear of mine (going to a wedding with many distant relatives). Fourth , I was asked to sing a solo at an upcoming concert. It is interesting to me that I can feel success in so many parts of my life and it feels so good.

I believe we often fear success more than we fear failure. Let's face it, success can be scary and intimidating. This is because with success, and the recognition that we can excel, comes the expectation that we can repeat this achievement. And with expectation, comes the fear of disappointing and failing. Sometimes, we actually sabotage success to avoid these fears. It is difficult and challenging to embrace success and these expectations. It takes confidence and courage to say, "I did it" and "I am worthy of praise for my actions". However, having enough self-esteem to recognize what you do well is a sign of self-acceptance and self-appreciation. And this, more often than not, motivates us to seek new challenges and inevitably reach new levels of success.

Success is different for everyone but acknowledge and embrace your success. It is when we are able to see our own successes that we grow and take one step closer to fulfilling our greatest potential.

People

"Great minds discuss ideas, average minds discuss events, small minds discuss people."
- Hyman Rickover

People have much to teach us. People frequently come in and out of our lives each and every day, each one touching us differently and making some impact on us. These people come in all shapes and sizes and are from all walks of life. Some people play more significant roles in our lives than others. Some people hinder us and seem to be obstacles in our paths. Sometimes, people affect us without our awareness. However, I believe every single person in our life serves a purpose: to show us something, to help us, to model for us; essentially, to teach us lessons in sharing, giving, patience, and understanding. The litany of lessons is really endless.

Sometimes I question why certain people, those annoying arrogant types who so easily get under one's skin, enter my life. I get frustrated and angry and I react and fight their every word. Yet, I slowly realize each time I come into contact with someone I just don't "get" that there's something to be learned. In the words of Carl Jung, "Everything that irritates us about others can lead to an understanding of ourselves". Whether that person's idiosyncrasies are meant to teach us patience or empathy, or understanding, the fact is that person who appears to be so irritating is still a person with feelings, thoughts, and experiences that make him or her that way.

Conversely, they are also those people in our lives who are nothing but pure blessings. They are boisterous, exuberant, rays of sunshine who give us energy and boost our confidence simply by being who they are. I have several people like this in my life, and I am grateful. These people really glow and I just love being in their presence. They listen to me. They are patient and kind. They are enthusiastic. They care.

We may feel we are sometimes better off without people. By ourselves there is less chance of being disappointed; there is less pain; there is more independence; and there is definitely more freedom. Yet while isolation and seclusion may temporarily feel "freeing", this "freedom" will ultimately lead to loneliness and depression. We need people.

People need to be a priority in our lives. People, regardless of who they are, serve a purpose: to teach us about ourselves, about themselves, and about the world.

Dreaming

"If one is lucky, a solitary fantasy can totally transform one million realities."
— Maya Angelou

I love to dream...BIG. Often I sit and, without any limitations or conditions, I allow myself to think of all the things I want to achieve and all the success I know I will attain. Sometimes I catch myself thinking pessimistically. Thoughts such as, "I'll never do that," or "I'll never be that fortunate" fill my head. And then I stop myself, correct these thoughts, and affirm myself with this key phrase: "I can do anything I set my mind to doing because I have the power from within." We all have the power, courage, and gifts to reach our greatest potential. The difference between dreamers and achievers is that achievers have the vision and the mission to reach the vision. You need a plan of action. Ask yourself this critical question: "If you could do anything and be anyone without the fear of failure, what would you do, and who would you be?" And after asking yourself this question, go for it; just do it!

Often we dream with self-imposed rules. I encourage you to dream HUGE - with money, talent, time, and people as NO object. It is, after all, your dream. I have always dreamed about singing professionally, traveling around the world, helping people in a third world country, obtaining my masters degree, and writing books. Years ago I did not believe that I could ever do any of these things. But as I grew and became more confident in myself and in my abilities, I came to understand that the only person that could prevent me from doing these things, fulfilling these dreams, was I. I chose not to sabotage myself and I have now reached many of these dreams.

Allow yourself to dream. Let your mind go free. And then challenge yourself to make your dreams a reality. Why? This is because you can. Realize the dreams you've put aside or even given up on and rethink the possibilities of reaching them.

Community

"There can be no vulnerability without risk; there can be no community without vulnerability; there can be no peace, and ultimately no life, without community."
- M. Scott Peck

Community is togetherness - a group of individuals who can share, give, love, feel, and grow together. Community is a support network, being there for one another and a place to call "home".

Community is manifested in a variety of ways: in a family, in a choir, in a school, in a business, or in a club. No matter what the location, the common threads that join these people together, (similar traits, attitudes, interests, and goals), are evident.

Without community and without a feeling of belonging and connection, one can feel lost, isolated, alone, hopeless, desperate, and even depressed. We all yearn to feel needed, belonged, cared for, and appreciated. There is no greater joy than this sense of affirmation and purpose. Community sustains us in bad times and allows us to celebrate in good times. Community is essential to healthy living.

There is something magical about being a part of something beyond yourself. Nothing compares to feeling as though we belong, that we are appreciated, and that we are here for a specific reason. Let's celebrate our community.

Diversity

"Everything that irritates us about others can lead to an understanding of ourselves."

— Carl Jung

I am often astonished at how different people are. Even within the same family, everyone is his or her own person with unique feelings, thoughts, experiences and responses to the world. We should view these differences as a good thing. There is much strength in diversity. It is by drawing on peoples' talents that we help to bring out their very best. In any group there is an array of gifts and talents. The key is to focus on the positive things people offer - not the negative. It is easy to complain about differences. Sometimes, we feel that if we were all the same, we would "get" each other so much more. We would certainly all understand the world in the same way and there would, of course, be harmony. But this manner of thinking is detrimental. Even when people are raised in the exact same way, (the same food, the same people, the same environment, and the same experiences), there are differences. This is because we are meant to be different.

I am learning to appreciate each person I know as an individual with unique characteristics. I know I am not meant to befriend everyone and that I will bond with certain people better than others. But I challenge myself each and every day to accept all dimensions of people.

It is alright to agree to disagree. Not everyone will see eye to eye and not everyone will like you. It is a waste of time (not to mention energy) to try to please everybody all of the time.

Knowing that differences are warranted will mean much less stress and frustration for you.

Is it not our responsibility to learn how to accept and embrace differences in people? The challenge and the blessing in relationships is to see people for who they really are and to accept all of their qualities.

There is so much strength in diversity. It is not a question of working toward making everyone the same but, rather, working to understand and appreciate the differences.

Self-acceptance

"Appreciate yourself so that others will too."

- Unknown

It is true: we are our own worst critics. We readily cut ourselves down, judging, self-deprecating and criticizing our looks, our actions, and our lives. It is easy to do. Moreover, self-destruction is a hard habit to break. The other day I was mortified when I looked at some pictures of myself. I ripped myself apart until I felt incredibly weak, vulnerable, and depressed. I couldn't get over how horrible I felt I looked. And if that weren't bad enough, I then felt guilty for being so shallow. These negative thoughts prevented me from enjoying some events and people for that day. I just could not get over it.

Why is it so difficult to accept and love ourselves unconditionally? How do we learn to care for our whole selves - the good and the bad? How do we come to be satisfied with our beautiful selves? I believe that the first step towards self-acceptance is self-awareness. Get to know yourself, completely. Ask yourself questions, challenge your beliefs and values, probe into your motivation, your desires, and your behaviors. Be honest. Be real. Be completely open. After all, you are your most valued commodity. The more thorough your reflecting can be, the better you will understand who you are and what you stand for.

The second step to self-acceptance is self-appreciation. After your "inquisition", think about all your good qualities. It is easy to condemn yourself, compare yourself to others, and feel less than adequate. You may think you got the short end of the deal. But by being kind to yourself, complimenting yourself, making a habit of positive self-talk, and focusing on what you do well, you will develop a new liking of yourself. Do not consume yourself criticizing. Uplift and encourage the beautiful, intelligent, worthy being you are. Be your best self.

Self-acceptance is no easy task but by getting to know yourself and by appreciating your unique talents and abilities, you will learn how to appreciate all you have to offer.

Thoughts

"I think therefore I am."
>   - Descartes

Our thoughts affect our actions. What we believe is who we are. This is not a difficult concept to grasp. Let me expound.

If you hate your boss and think he or she is arrogant, selfish, authoritarian and unfair, chances are your body language and attitude are going to be manifestations of these thoughts. You may not get too close. You may not smile. You may just look annoyed or disinterested. Whatever your reasons for thinking these negative thoughts (and they may well be very legitimate reasons), it is certainly true to say your beliefs about your boss are influencing your behavior.

If we think angry thoughts we become angry people. Conversely, if we think joyful thoughts we become joyful. Have you ever noticed how smiling (even if it is forced and fake) automatically makes you feel happier?

It is important to try to be the best person you can be and this requires you to have a loving attitude toward people: an attitude filled with kindness, compassion, understanding, and acceptance. A positive attitude and a positive behavior begins with positive thoughts. It is our job to find the good in people and focus on their positive traits. Extracting the positive attributes eliminates (or at least overpowers) the negative. We need to make a conscious choice to be aware of our thinking and correct harmful thinking patterns. Every negative thought can be adjusted to a more hopeful thought. We need to think good thoughts on purpose and believe this will help improve our disposition.

Good thinking requires effort. We need to be aware of our thoughts and make the necessary adjustments, knowing our thoughts are reflected in our actions.

Opportunity

"It is only when we truly know and understand that we have a limited time on earth - and that we have no way of knowing when our time is up - that we will begin to live each day to the fullest, as if it was the only one we had."

- Elizabeth Kubler-Ross

The world is filled with opportunities. We can do anything, be anybody and go anywhere. Opportunity is ours for the taking. Sometimes, I wonder why I don't do more - why I restrict my thinking and, therefore, my actions to a small little world. Perhaps I am held back by fear - fear of feeling or even fear of succeeding. Sometimes, I feel overwhelmed and debilitated by life. Sometimes, I am just not motivated.

My challenge to you (and to myself) is to change your paradigm. Change the way you view the world from one of restriction, barriers, problems, and "I can's" to one without limitations and obstacles: a mindset that is open to change, flexible, and without boundaries. A mind that knows no bounds. Isn't that, after all, why we are here? To do the most we can and to be our best?

We could die tomorrow. There are no guarantees that we will live to see our next birthday or our next sunset. We are definitely not immortal beings. Shouldn't we seize the day without hesitation and without regrets?

Stop making excuses. Stop listening to the negative voices. Stop feeding off fear and go for it. Live your life the best you can. Do the things you've always wanted to do - not because you should, but because you can. Go for it!

Disappointment

"He who expects much can expect little."
> - Gabriel Garcia Marquez

"Live is so constructed, that the event does not, cannot, will not, match the expectation."
> - Charlotte Bronte

Did you ever notice how almost without fail if you have high expectations you have greater chances of being disappointed? For some reason, every time I am excited about an event and plan it out in my mind; (what I will wear, who will be there, how I will feel), the reality never seems to match the fantasy. I tend to overemphasize what could happen and this overemphasis exceeds what does happen. Disappointment and feelings of being let down are inevitable. Yet, ironically, some of my fondest memories are times when I had no preconceived notions of how something would unfold - times when I was completely spontaneous and relaxed. I am not suggesting one live life without expectations, for fear of being disappointed. I am suggesting that perhaps too much thought and analysis detracts us from important life events. We miss out because we are busy planning the details. By allowing life to just happen, and by surrendering our inherent need to have power and be in control, we may enjoy ourselves more.

    I think it is also important to note that disappointment is part life but that we must be careful that we do not allow it to rule our lives. How much of human life is lost in waiting? We spend too much time focusing on the past and planning ahead for the future and we thus miss out on the moments at present. Sometimes, people will let us down, opportunities will pass us by, or we will fail ourselves. But we need to learn from these experiences and not become too cynical. The more we understand that negative consequences are going to happen, the better equipped we will be to handle them and move forward.

Disappointments don't have to hold us back. They can be opportunities to learn and become stronger. I want to pump you up!

Passion

"Nothing great in this world has been accomplished without passion."
   - George Wilheim Friedrich Hegel

"If you don't know what your passion is, realize that one reason for your existence on earth is to find it."
            - Oprah Winfrey

   Find your passion - the one thing you love to do; what brings you complete joy; what you couldn't possibly live without doing. And hold on to it. Allow that passion to sustain you. Passion is all about listening to your heart and following your dreams.
   I am extremely passionate about several things: education, teaching, learning, studying, and singing. Not a day goes by where I do not think about

these precious areas of my life at least once. They bring me a lot of joy and contentment. They are all equally important to me. I live, I breathe, and I revel in these opportunities. I enjoy my passions and appreciate my gifts. I love to challenge myself and grow in these areas.

I know I am lucky to have such passion for singing and for education. I know many people live their entire lives without finding their true calling or without following this calling. Sometimes people are afraid of failing, other times they are afraid of succeeding. Some people lack the belief in their abilities. Others lack the tenacity to keep trying even when doors may shut on them.

Passion is the driving force, the energy, the excitement, and the charisma that propels us to do what we do: the living, breathing spirit within us. Passion is our heart speaking to us and telling us to simply "go for it" and to "just do it". Passion is feeling and, by bringing passion into our lives, we allow our true selves to be heard and felt.

Some people have passion for sports, people, nature, politics, writing, cooking, researching, art, dancing, children, or business. Whatever your passion is, be true to yourself and allow it to emerge from within you.

Find your passion in life. Follow it. Allow it to motivate you, to challenge you, and to push you to grow. Passion will bring new meaning to your life and help you to live the life you are meant to be living.

Happiness

"Happiness comes from the capacity to feel deeply, to enjoy simply, to think freely, to be needed."
- Storm Jameson

What does happiness mean to you? What does happiness mean to me? Being happy is the choice I make each day to see the good in my life. It is the enjoyment of being my true self. It is the harmony between what I think, what I say, and what I do. We are, after all, as happy as we make up our minds to be. Unhappiness is the choice we make to let life get us down and rob us of pleasures. We often look for contentment in all the wrong places. The number of people who consider themselves happy has been declining over the past thirty years.

Did you ever wonder what makes some people deliriously happy and others so painfully discontented? It is perhaps not so much a matter of life events but of disposition. With a good disposition and a positive outlook on life, one is much more prepared and well equipped to handle adversity. These fortunate ones can take any situation and turn it into a fulfilling, enriching learning experience. It is a fact that no matter who you are life is going to be turbulent, trying, and wearing. However, it is our response to the world and our perspective that will make all the difference.

When people depend on others for their happiness they may feel good temporarily. Yet, they are really deluding themselves into believing they are content. When this source of happiness fades or disappoints or cannot fulfill us, we are left destitute and, most likely, lonely. However, by depending on the sources within ourselves for our sole happiness, we learn to see that we have tremendous abilities and strengths to complete ourselves, to make us feel worthy and whole, and to provide us with our needs.

Happiness is completely in your power. Choose to be happy and see just how happy you will become. It is easy to find happiness in ourselves. It is impossible to find it elsewhere.

Fear

"Let me assert my firm beliefs that the only thing we have to fear is fear itself."
- Franklin D. Roosevelt

Fear of change. Fear of failure. Fear of the unknown. Fear of rejection. Fear of commitment. Fear of happiness. Fear of success. This plethora of common fears could go on forever. We all have fears, some rational, based on experience; most irrational, based on our imagination.

Have you ever become completely incapacitated and overwhelmed by a fear? You spend endless nights thinking about how you can avoid a situation or a person, perhaps even devising a strategy to get out of a commitment. You waste an abundance of energy worrying and wondering. And when you finally face the fear (that is, if you find the courage), you realize you completely overreacted. You then feel a sense of shame and guilt and perhaps some pride of accomplishment, satisfaction, and most certainly some relief!

The point is, our minds often get the best of us and concoct horror stories that allow our fears to prevent us from even trying. Our fears may keep us from meeting new people, hold us back from speaking our minds, or keep us in a job we absolutely detest. By giving our fears power over us, we are held back from learning, growing and becoming our very best.

I have learned that there is nothing holding me back in life except for me. I create my own barriers that prevent me from succeeding and achieving my goals. I have also come to realize that fear is a waste of time and energy because what I fear is usually nothing at all. Unfortunately, fear is often my excuse for not trying.

Overcoming fear is like overcoming a battle. It takes some time and effort. But make the effort to confront your fears and embrace all that comes with these fears. Addressing trepidation is the key that unlocks the door to a world of excitement, adventure, and opportunity.

We always fear the worst but we must remember that by challenging our fears we will grow and become all we are meant to be.

Growth

"Each step forward makes me stronger for the next step."

- Gandhi

You can only grow when you are willing to take risks and accept change. You can only grow by moving (even if you are petrified and filled with uncertainty). It is true to say that nobody ever got anywhere by harboring stagnation and enjoying the sameness of everyday. We have to push forward and grow.

Growth is development. We grow as we live and as we encounter new experiences. We also feel our emotions as we meet new people and as we learn. Growth is acknowledging you are continuously becoming a refined individual. As you grow, you become.

And as you become, you emerge. Growth is the release of your unlimited potential.

    Growth is often stunted; this is frustrating. We try to change. We want to change. And yet, the reality is we are not changing! However, growth seems to just happen, often without our awareness, and usually when we expect it the least.

Take one day at a time as you grow and become a person willing to grow. Live within the hours of the day.

Attitude

"The greatest discovery of my generation is that human beings can alter their lives by altering their attitudes."
- William James

Attitude is everything! My positive attitude comes from my dad, and I am eternally grateful. No matter what grief he had to bear, no matter how tough life seemed to be, no matter how financially strapped we were, my dad had a positive outlook. He was able to hold his optimistic attitude, knowing everything would work out and that tomorrow would be a brighter, newer day. Not only did he have this optimism and enthusiasm within his own being, but through his words and actions he was able to communicate this optimism to the rest of the family. This sense of hope and promise gave us the energy and impetus to keep going. Optimism sustained and saved us.

Again, attitude is everything. If you display a positive attitude and think positive thoughts you will not only be able to see the good in people but extract this good from them. If you hope for the best, you are likely going to get it. It really is that simple.

A positive attitude is great for yourself and for those around you. Everybody benefits from a joyous, hopeful spirit. A positive attitude is contagious. By giving people the joyful gift of optimism, you are starting a fire that will burn for some time. People who feel your positivity will tend to pass it on and on. And on it will travel.

It is all too easy to be negative. It is easy to see what is wrong with your life, other people, and the world. It takes time and practice to be positive and see what is right. A positive attitude reaps positive energy. This positive energy promotes positivity - healing, transforming, and conducting love.

You have a choice: to be positive or negative; the former perhaps requiring more effort (making more impact on others, helping make the world a happier place) and practise, yet creating more happiness and reaping more rewards.

Goals

"Most people would succeed in small things, if they were not troubled with great ambitions."
— Henry Wadsworth Longfellow

I have always been a goal-oriented person. I enjoy dreaming of goals, making a plan, taking small steps, acting and, ultimately, achieving my goals. Nothing is more satisfying to me than successfully attaining the goals I set forth for myself. I have both short-term and long-term goals - daily, weekly, and yearly plans of how to reach these successes. I feel that my identity and self-worth is not only defined by but sustained by my ability to establish goals.

Goal-setting has many benefits. First, it keeps me organized. I am able to see what I want to get done and then do it. Second, it keeps me fresh and motivated. Reviewing my goals, I am able to view my journey: where I was, where I am, and where I have yet to go. Finally, goal-setting helps me feel good about myself. I feel my goals give me a sense of purpose and belonging. I know that I am acting with integrity; I do exactly what I say I am going to do.

If I did not set goals, I think I would end up doing the same thing over and over. I know that I would feel frustrated with myself, not to mention disorganized. And I would most likely not be where I want to be. Without goals, I would lack direction and purpose.

Some people argue that goal-setting is too time-consuming. I would argue the opposite. It takes little time and really saves you an abundance of your future time. Start slowly, perhaps listing a few goals stated within a timeline. Then, add goal-setting tactics: daily, monthly, yearly lists, short and long term plans, and rewards for your achievement. It is never too late. Like anything, it takes time and practise. Remember, there is so much joy in seeing and participating in the process of goal-setting. The process, instead of instant gratification, is what is incredibly rewarding.

Without being too rigid or obsessed, start making goals and taking small steps to reach these goals. You will be amazed at what you can do with a little planning and organization.

Self-discovery

"Figuring out who you are is the whole point of human experience."
- Anna Quindlen

To let ourselves be known to others means we have to know ourselves first. What do you believe? What do you value? What do you stand for? What is your purpose in this world? Where do you fit in? Learning to ask these questions and learning to reveal ourselves is a pertinent life lesson.

Although you may have learned to hide your feelings and keep your thoughts and opinions to yourself in order to protect yourself from harm and keep safe, you must realize what you are missing out on. Being vulnerable to yourself and thus to others is an essential step to being whole. By finding people whom you can trust and by revealing little bits about yourself, you can eventually learn to disclose yourself and be content in relationships. Slowly, you can learn to open up and be known.

Take the time to know and understand yourself. Be patient and trust that in time you will be able to discover yourself and then disclose yourself to loved ones surrounding you.

Self-care

"When you practise extreme self-care, you wrap yourself in an energy that creates miracles in your life and in the lives of those around you."

- Shirley Anderson

Self-care is doing what is necessary to feel good about yourself and to be a healthy, happy, balanced individual. I once felt that self-care was selfish. I mistook self-care for greed, vanity, and narcissism. I believed that taking time for myself and taking care of myself was wasted time.

However, I have long since learned the necessity of self-care and, of course, the benefits. Self-care can be whatever you want it to be as long as you enjoy it, indulge in it, and benefit from it. For some, self-care is journaling and the opportunity to reflect on life and express one's thoughts and feelings. For others, self-care is not any specific act but general care and maintenance of one's self: speaking kind words, relaxing, and being good to yourself. You'll be astounded by how much more you can accomplish and how much more you will have to offer loved ones in a given day when you take the time to nourish your spirit first and care for your needs.

We all have the power, knowledge, and ability to do what we need to do for our personal happiness. Nobody knows what is best for you as much as you do, even if you do not yet have the awareness of your needs. Listen to yourself and act accordingly. Relax, take walks, read, meditate, spend time with family, and enjoy nature's blessings. There is no book of rules or formula match our needs. Unfortunately, life did not come with an instruction book. But fortunately, we have the "answers" within us. We need to listen, trust, and have the courage to ask the questions.

We have to accept the notion of giving ourselves what we want and need. It is really okay to care for and love ourselves.

Encouragement

"You maximize other people's potential when you nurture their spirit. And you nurture another person's spirit when you encourage him or her. Encouraging words are the legs that nature walks on."
- Unknown

Encouragement is contagious. When somebody uplifts you with praise and with kind and promising words, the impact is astounding. Not only will you feel the renewed sense of hope but an impetus to move forward and to fight on. Additionally, you will most likely encourage somebody else because you know how good it feels and what a difference it makes to your outlook on life. Thus, a chain reaction begins.

The other night, I received an enormous compliment when a mere stranger took time to pull me aside to say, "thank you" for being so genuine, positive, and warm. This individual said that I made him feel better and that I was a refreshing change to some cynical, skeptical people he happens to meet. What a great compliment! I realized how much effect a few thoughtful words can have. It took a little time and effort and a little thought. And yet, I gave somebody hope and joy.

We all have the power to build people up just as we have the power to put people down. We must use this knowledge about our power wisely. We need to encourage each other. Tell people what a great job they do, what a difference they make, and just how much they mean to you. We have tremendous power to help people along the way! And it is amazing how things work because just when you think you are without purpose and belonging, an encouraging word will come your way. After all, you get what you give!

People must help and encourage one another. Why? Because we can! Remember how good you feel when you are embraced and encouraged.

Discipline

"When you stay focused and keep a commitment you create momentum, and momentum creates momentum."
- Rich Fettke

Discipline is the combination of the performance of daily tasks, the trust that the goal will be attained, the understanding that our behaviors have consequences, the undertaking of responsibility for our actions, the willingness to work for what we want, and the courage to learn, accept, and practise new behaviors.

Discipline is hard work. Discipline may evoke feelings of insecurity, fear, vulnerability, frustration, confusion, and uncertainty. We may not always see the purpose or the results. We may feel stuck an in a state of inertia. Yet, the rewards of discipline are tenfold. Often with discipline, come feelings of achievement, success, progress, growth, responsibility, and development. Sowing the seeds of discipline reaps immeasurable rewards.

We need discipline to experience structure, a sense of challenge, and a sense of new found security.

Surrender to discipline. Put in the time. Do the work. Trust the purpose. And see what results emerge.

Boundaries

"Audacity augments courage; hesitation, fear."

> - Publius Syrus

Today I was able to establish and maintain my boundaries. And I have to say, I feel ecstatic for doing so. I am the type of person to say "yes" to everybody's demands; a people-pleaser, if you will. I am not certain why. I know I like to share what I have and I know I like to help people. I also know that I yearn to be accepted and I fear letting people down. It is for all these reasons that I have difficulty with boundaries.

Normally, people ask me for a favor and I just agree, even if it means sacrificing my time, energy, or personal well-being. However, I am learning this is wrong for several reasons. First, by not taking care of myself, I am hurting myself. The more I practise self-care, the more I will have to offer. Secondly, if I help somebody out and do not really want to, I am helping with a bitter heart. I believe that if you do not act with pure intentions, this is worse than not acting at all. Lastly, lending a hand when I am really unable to do so means compromising myself, (who I am and what I stand for), and this is not healthy.

So, today, when told I was meant to do something, I was able to assertively stand up for myself, calmly and tactfully explain my feelings, and define my boundaries (as I felt they had been crossed). The result amazed me: the person respected my assertion and withdrew the request with much understanding. I was able to command the respect I deserved by not fulfilling the role of the "doormat".

I believe sacrifice is good sometimes. We are going to have to accommodate different people's needs. Sometimes, we'll have to put others' needs first. I think it is warranted. However, we must remember to take care of ourselves, speak our minds, and establish our limits; we must let people know what we will and will not do for them. By doing so, we are not being rude. We are being bold and setting boundaries.

Boundaries are healthy assertions of ourselves. We must make our boundaries evident and consistently adhere to them.

Peace

"Resolve conflict with your family and strengthen your relationships with loved ones."
- Joan Lunden

I was always told to "never go to bed angry" and to make peace with people. I think one of my biggest fears is that I will lose a loved one without being on good terms with that person. Sometimes after a quarrel or disagreement with a friend or family member, a guilty conscience forces me to query, "what if he or she died today?" A horrible thought to say the least, but one that resides within me for a reason: to get me to say I am sorry, to work things out, and to ask for forgiveness. It is not about being right or wrong because sometimes being right and "winning" a fight means losing the respect and trust of someone special - losing a valuable connection. I have learned to make peace with people frequently and consistently because it is the right thing to do. By making peace, I feel good. I feel harmonious with others, and I feel the benefits are endless. Peace with others brings me peace of mind and inner joy.

    The effort to make peace begins with one individual. Thinking on a larger scale, such as world peace, is really no different. Change begins with one whether we are talking about peace of mind, peace in a classroom, peace in a city, or peace in a country. Making amends, seeking forgiveness, and taking responsibility for our actions starts with an individual who has integrity and courage and can set aside pride to make things right.

Peace on every level is attained with the boldness and audacity to do the right thing.

Proactivity

"I have seen who I want to be. I must act to make it so."

- Greg Anderson

If you want to be happy, you must create a life that is conducive to happiness. If you want friends, you must befriend people. If you want forgiveness, you must be willing to forgive. Life is a transfer of energy - you get what you give just as you take what you need. So instead of complaining about what is missing in your life and what you do not have, you may wish to ask what it is you can give and what it is that others need from you.

You reap what you sow. It is true. How can one expect to be content with one's life when one self-sabotages with unhappy thoughts, negative people, and detrimental situations? If you sow unhappiness, you will reap unhappiness. Sow what you want, what you need, and be amazed at the result.

I have found I set my life up for achievement. I am a very goal-oriented person, to say the least. I have goals on a large spectrum, (dreams, if you will), and I break these larger goals into smaller, daily goals. Slowly, day by day and week by week, my activities and actions work up to reaching my bigger goals. I am often amazed and ever so astounded at how much I achieve. Yet, I shouldn't be too astounded because I definitely set myself up for making my dreams come true. I am organized, I surround myself with goodhearted, positive people, and I consistently reflect on my actions to ensure continuous quality improvement and development. There are no guarantees that my actions will yield success but the chances are good, or better than good. I find that there is always something to be learned.

I am a firm believer in development and progression. You are not born great at any one activity (most of us, anyway). You must practise and work on the things you want to master. This can pertain to a sport, an instrument, or simply character. It takes effort and time.

Take action! If you want to be happy, you must sow the seeds of happiness. If you want to be successful, you must sow the seeds of success.

Clarity

"In my life's chain of events, nothing was accidental. Everything happened according to an inner need."
— Hannah Senesh

Clarity is the ability to see people and the world as they are. Of course, we all have lenses and see things from our unique perspectives. But we also can have the clarity within our own frame of reference.

Sometimes, all we can see is today. Sometimes, this is all we can handle and this is enough. Often, when we see this so narrowly, we may feel confused and lost. We may also feel disconnected. Our limited perspective yields limited vision. Yet, we must learn to understand we have tunnel vision and a lack of clarity for a reason.

Perhaps, there is a lesson we must learn. Maybe we need to do some more work on ourselves. Maybe we need to get back to basics and question, challenge, and really contemplate our purpose.

I have learned that clarity comes when we have mastered various lessons. Clarity emerges when it is time. We must trust that our experiences are not a mistake and that we go through things so that we can grow. There is preparation for clarity.

Only when the time is right, and only when we are ready to grow, will we be able to see the "big picture". As we grow and learn, we come to understand how our experiences fit into the grand scheme of things. Finally, we can see from a broader perspective and appreciate the steps that brought us to this place. We are being changed, healed, transformed, developed, and reshaped at levels much deeper than we can imagine. We are being prepared for our time of clarity. Answers, direction, and clarity will come.

Clarity and insight emerge when we have learned the lessons we are meant to learn. We must trust experiences even when we cannot see why they are happening.

Emotions

"Today, I will allow myself to recognize and accept whatever feelings pass through me. Without shame, I will tune in to the emotional part of myself."
- Melody Beattie

Our emotions are a huge part of us. We are, by nature, emotional beings. Our feelings let people know when we are happy and excited, when we are angry and frustrated, and even when we are tired and apathetic. Our emotions are communicated in what we say, how we say it, and our overall body language.

Our body entire is made up several dimensions: emotional, physical, intellectual, social and spiritual. Emotions are a vital part of us. If our emotions are such a grand part of us, why do so many of us struggle so profusely to feel them and, moreover, why are so many of us so evidently challenged to communicate them? Why do we feel such a need to hide them, distort them, and make them "appropriate"? Why do certain situations evoke such emotions? Why do we get so emotional sometimes and not other times?

I believe feeling our emotions are essential. I also believe it is a true challenge, especially if we have learned not to feel. Letting yourself deal with your emotions means several things. First, you have to be ready and willing to honestly examine yourself and your life. Second, you have to be willing to work at acknowledging and accepting your feelings. You must be patient and practise. Third, you must learn to communicate your emotions to yourself and then to others.

The feeling component of ourselves is so important. It allows us to show fear, be sad, get excited, and share pain. Our emotions may appear to have a life of their own: persuading us here, pushing us there, prompting and provoking us to act and bringing us down. We must seek the emotional part of ourselves and then, with honesty, openness, and understanding, share that part.

Open up the emotional part of yourself. Acknowledge and accept your feelings. Our emotions connect us to our physical, intellectual, and spiritual selves. Keep the connection.

Surrender

"Make a decision to turn our will and our lives over to the care of God as we understood Him."
- Step Three of Al-Anon

It is my contention that surrendering may be one of the most difficult acts. Surrendering to people, circumstances, and life is not giving up but giving to. It means giving up the need to control and giving in to the idea you are omnipotent. Surrender is trusting that what is meant to be will be. It is the most challenging, yet rewarding decision to be made.

In trying times when you feel lost, hopeless, and destitute, the option of surrendering and giving up "control" seems ludicrous. Yet, when we surrender, we receive the gift of release: feelings of fear and anxiety and uncertainty are released and we no longer feel that inherent, driving need to control and "fix" what is broken. Surrender is the process that enables us to take the next step in our circumstance and move forward. Surrender is a highly emotional, spiritual experience. Surrendering is also the opportunity to become empowered. We become new, better, more effective people, with a fresh outlook on our lives. We live in to our potential.

Surrendering is allowing the plan to unfold. It is a time to give in to what we are feeling and experiencing and encounter renewal and growth. There is much power in surrender.

Healing

"We should learn not to grow impatient with the slow healing process of time..."
> - Joshua Loth Liebman

The body has an amazing ability to heal itself. The body operates like a well-oiled machine. Uninterrupted, it functions extremely efficiently. All too often we believe we can speed up the process. I am very guilty of this. If I develop a physical injury, I will deny it and resist treatment. I'll rest little, use it a lot and, more often than not, my injury prolongs and sometimes worsens. It is challenging to trust that the body's healing process will do the work and overcome the pain. It is hard to believe the body knows what to do. We fail to surrender to the body.

However, time and time again our bodies prove they can and do function if left alone to do the work.

Healing takes time and patience. But healing will happen. It is sometimes "painful" to simply let things happen. Yet, doing nothing is often the best thing for us. Healing takes time and is a process not to be interrupted. Generally, we cannot rush or speed up this natural process. Let healing come. It will. Attract it. Accept it. Breathe in. Exhale. Let go of your fear, reluctance, hurt, and doubt. Let healing enter you and do the work. Rest. Relax. Do what you can. And then let the healing process transpire.

Allow the healing energy to flow through you. Let healing do its job. Healing is available to you. Believe it and just see the miracle take place.

Vulnerability

"I've learned that the more vulnerable I allow myself to be, the more in control of myself I really am."
- Anonymous

Letting yourself be vulnerable entails trusting people, opening yourself up to others and letting yourself be known. Vulnerability is a risk and courage is mandatory. Being vulnerable is sharing of yourself, admitting your imperfections and idiosyncrasies and being open to the possibility of love and acceptance. The person you choose to be vulnerable to may betray you, disappoint you or even take advantage of you. Being vulnerable is, in my opinion, is an extremely courageous act. I have not yet mastered this act.

I let people get to know me slowly and with a lot of caution. This is because as a child I learned not to trust and to keep quiet. Feelings were not encouraged in our household and I was always expected to be the "strong one". I had to put on a brave front when facing the world. Therefore, I find it difficult to trust and to depend on people. I expect they will let me down and disappoint me. I am very "independent" and "self-reliant". I am also very fearful of rejection and judgment. Often times, this also leaves me not only alone but also lonely. I let people get close to me but not too close. There always comes a point in time where that barrier I have constructed around me just will not come down. Or rather, I do not allow it to come down because of my fears.

I am fully aware of my inability to let myself be vulnerable. I am also aware this "inability" is my choice right now. It is my away of hiding from potential pain. It is how I keep myself safe. For now, I am allowing myself to be this way. And I know I must work through my fear and eventually be vulnerable. I will take small steps: communicate my feelings, let people in to my life slowly, and, eventually, allow others to see all of me, in full color, whole and accessible. This will take time. Yet, I see this culmination of small steps as a challenge.

Vulnerability is the ability to be known, to express your wants and needs, to share your feelings and to enjoy the freedom to be exactly who you are at all times. Practise being appropriately vulnerable - sharing all dimensions of yourself with people whom you trust and respect.

Timing

"If we could untangle the mysteries of life and unravel the energies which run through the world; if we could evaluate correctly the significance of passing events; if we could measure the struggles, dilemmas, and aspirations of mankind, we could find that nothing is born out of time. Everything comes at its appointed moment."
- Joseph R. Sizoo

Time is constant. It goes on regardless of circumstances. Time does not merely take on a life of its own; time is a life of its own. Yet, even with this knowledge we want to change time, depending on our lives. We may find we are always dissatisfied with time. When we are having fun and happy with the moment, we want time to stand still. When we are deep in sorrow and feeling life has the best of us, we cannot wait for time to pass. Speed up, slow down, stand still - time will not. Time really does act independently of us.

Timing is everything. There is a time and a season for every moment and every memory. Everything happens for a reason. Timing, even if we may not believe it, is perfect. Wait until the time is right. Both acting too soon and acting too late are self-defeating behaviors. Both are ineffective. When the time is right, and you will know when it is, act and do what needs to be done.

Be patient that everything happens at the exact moment it is meant to happen. Time is impeccable.

Celebration

"Find joy in your life everyday by appreciating the simple things."
- Unknown

Celebrate your successes, your growth and your accomplishments. There must be time to celebrate - time to look back and reflect and see just how far you've come, time to enjoy where you are at in your life, and time to be with people who can share your excitement and happiness about who you are. Without time to pause and acknowledge all you have accomplished, you may burn out and miss the whole purpose of why you do what you do. Part of the benefits of celebrating are that one is afforded the opportunity to relax and then potentially motivated to push forward.

I am one known for skipping celebration. It is always my intention to work towards fulfilling my vision and then take at least a few moments to revel in the glory of my achievements. Unfortunately, I find that no sooner do I reach my goals, do I quickly begin new projects, without taking any time at marvel at my feats. I think that deep down I may feel that if I slow down, I will not want to get moving again. Or I feel that if I accept my achievements, I will lose them. However, I have realized it is beneficial to celebrate. And it is rude not to recognize what you have done and share. Celebrating what we do and who we are is not being arrogant or conceited - it is merely showing gratitude.

Celebrate your achievements, your relationships and your journey. Celebrate who you are - your life!

Denial

"There are people who make things happen, those who watch what happens, and those who wonder what happened."
- Unknown

Denial is a sneaky characteristic. It tends to take on its own identity. When we are in denial, we obviously neither recognize nor admit to this defense mechanism, which protects us and keeps us safe and, at the same time, has the potential to debilitate and destroy us. It is only after we acknowledge and deal with our denial concerns that we come to realize what we were doing and how we were erroneously behaving.

Denial is a defense mechanism that functions to protect us and keep us safe in the face of adversity, pain and danger. Denial helps us to make reality more tolerable. Denial is a powerful tool. We cannot underestimate its ability to cloud our vision and distort the truth. Denial is a fantasy reality. It is a defense, a survival device, a coping behavior, an enemy and, often times, our best friend.

The advantage of denial is that it protects us. It helps us survive our circumstances and live the best we can at a given moment in time. It allows us to hide from situations too painful to deal with. The disadvantage of denial is that it also hides our feelings and prevents us from really confronting our pain and discomfort. However, denial is something of which we are not always aware.

Slowly, with awareness and practise, we can see our reliance on denial and then slowly begin breaking through our use of this mechanism. The goal, of course, is being able to accept reality as it is. Denial is like a blanket we use to wrap around ourselves to keep warm and help us feel secure. However, by learning to feel safe and warm by confronting and managing your emotions, you are participating in the healing process.

Understand that denial is a form of codependency - it helps you function and survive. Also understand denial is a distortion of reality. Face the facts when you are ready and feeling safe by dealing with your feelings. Move through denial and overcome the need to hold on to the need to live this way.

Perspective

"What lies behind us and what lies before us are tiny matters compared to what lies within us."
- Ralph Waldo Emerson

Sometimes we need a wake-up call (or several wake-up calls) to gain perspective. We may go through hard, troubling times and find ourselves complaining, negative, and downright miserable with our situation. We are cynical and dissatisfied until we learn of a good friend faced with a sudden bout with cancer or the loss of a loved one. We are busy, tired, and grumpy until someone we know is faced with unemployment. We are rude and careless with our words until we realize the impact we are making on others. Suddenly, we can only think to empathize with the people around us, care for them and spend time with them. Our busy schedule is put on hold, without thought or hesitation. We make ourselves available because we now have new perspective on the trivialness of our problems. We gain insight into the "big picture", the fragility of our time on earth, and the preciousness of time.

We now can make each and every day count. We can find great joy in the little things. We can value the special moments, all of the special moments. We can treasure the good times.

Losing perspective is common. We are so consumed with ourselves and with the frivolities within our own existence, we fail to see the world from a systemic point of view. In other words, we don 't see what's happening outside of ourselves: starving children in Africa, war in the Middle East, destruction and poverty in our cities and pain and suffering within our own homes.

    I am definitely not saying we have to suffer in order to appreciate our lives. I wouldn't wish harm on anyone. But I am saying that by expanding our minds and gaining accurate perspective on ourselves, our relationships and our life concerns, we are better able to understand the world as a whole, and why events unfold as they do.

From what perspective do you view the world? Is your perspective accurate? Check yourself - your beliefs, values, and priorities - in order to gain some perspective of the grand scheme of things.

Boredom

"Boredom is the gateway to peace."
                - Thomas Lenoard

    Boredom is a difficult notion to embrace let alone "enjoy". I have always felt boredom is a sure sign of laziness and lack of initiative. I would plan my days down to the minute in every effort to avoid having that dreaded "embarrassing" moment of having nothing to do.

    One the one hand, boredom can be viewed as a mismanagement of time, a cessation of inertia, a lack of ideas or a time of nothingness. On the other hand, boredom can be peace and tranquility. Our stimulus-filled, energetic, overly busy society has forgotten, or rather neglected, that there are many advantages in boredom; there is the art of silence, the joy of breathing and relaxing and the utmost pleasure of deep reflection.

Sometimes, we do not need to "do" anything. We can just be. And if this is deemed "boredom", then so be it. It is through this time of boredom that we may have our greatest moments of insight and peace.

We can grow from our times of boredom.

Perfection

"Love yourself first and everything else falls into line."
> - Unknown

    Our society not only shows us perfection but also demands if from us: our bodies, our hair, our makeup and our clothes. There is so much focus placed on perfection and such great pressure to be nothing but, it is no wonder we constantly feel unworthy and never quite "good enough".

    We have to realize that perfection does not exist. This is because we are human. And being human means we have faults, weaknesses, struggles, and idiosyncrasies. We have to allow ourselves to make mistakes, get off track sometimes and be corrected. Then we can learn and improve.

Furthermore, we cannot play the comparison game. By looking at others and believing they are perfect, we are disillusioning ourselves. And we will always come away feeling inferior. We are unique. We do not want to be just like everybody else, or we would have been created that way.

    Who we are is always good enough. We are okay, just as we come, without exception. Expecting perfection from ourselves or others slows down the growth process. When we stop expecting, we begin seeing. Self-love and self-acceptance promulgate growth.

Understand that perfection is nonexistent. Nobody is perfect and nobody should be. Learn to love your imperfect, wonderful, beautiful, miraculous self, forever.

Patience

"When you're waiting, you're not doing nothing. You're doing the most important something there is. You're allowing your soul to grow up. If you can't be still and wait, you can't become what God created you to be."
- Sue Monk Kidd

"Patience is a virtue." This is what my mom used to say to us as kids when we would be overflowing with excitement and begging for her to take us to the store, or make us lunch, or just read us a story. Without much thought about the value of her words, we continued to be completely impatient. Patience is a virtue. It is also a gift. Patient words, in collaboration with acceptance, surrender and gratitude, are priceless. You must practise patience, learn to wait and be calm.

Being patient is a learning experience in and of itself. We want what we want now. We expect instant gratification and fulfillment. Yet, sometimes by being forced to wait, we become that much more thankful when we are fulfilled. For example, there was a time when I really wanted specific direction for my life. I was at a crossroads, and I needed to decide what to do. I desperately sought a sign, a signal, an omen - anything that would point me to the right way. But I received nothing, not even the hint of an "answer". My patience was definitely being tested. I waited and waited some more until one day I was blessed with the perfect guidance, and I realized had I not been patient and forced to wait for that time of deliverance, I would not have learned the lessons that were taught in the meantime. Without learning these invaluable lessons, I would not have been as aware or appreciative of the "wisdom" I received that shed light on my path. Having patience paid off.

Be patient and wait for what will inevitably be delivered to you.

Prayer

"As a matter of fact, prayer is the only real action in full sense of the word, because prayer is the only thing that changes one's character. A change in character, or a change in soul, is a real change."

- Emmet Fox

There is power in prayer. There is enormous power in prayer. I am convicted. Yet, so often prayer is my last resort. I do everything I can to solve my own problems. I rely solely on myself to work through issues. And when I do not see results, I decide to pray. It is then that my prayer is answered, maybe not in the way I expected, but it is always answered.

Why do I not trust that my prayers will be heard? Why do I use prayer as a last resort? I believe it is a natural human flaw to lean on our own strength and knowledge. We feel omnipotent and wise beyond our years. We think, "of course I can do that. I'll work it out on my own", and "I can do anything I choose".

It is a humbling experience to bow down on bended knee and pray, especially when you have explored all other avenues first. This time of humility is a great moment of growth. Prayer and meditation are ways we take care of our spirits. Our spirits need attention so that we can change from within and connect to the rest of the world.

Pray for what you want and need. Pray for forgiveness, happiness, freedom, love, joy, kindness, healing, guidance and change. Then wait and listen and watch as miracles happen - because they always do.

We must believe that every prayer is heard and every prayer is answered, just as it should be.

Friendship

"Each friend represents a world in us, a world possibly not born until they arrive, and it is only by this meeting that a new world is born."
- Anais Nin

    I just finished a great book that offered advice about the real world in the form of "I wish I had known these things and now that I do, let me show you them." The author discussed a variety of issues from following your passion and appreciating the people you work with, to recognizing marriage is not always the "happily ever after" we are led to believe. The piece of advice given by this author that impacted me the most was this: "maintain your friendships, connect, and reconnect".

I grew up with a strong sense of establishing my independence. My mindset was one of "I am all right. I can do it all on my own." The funny thing is, I honestly believed this and, of course, every disappointment, mistrust, and let down reaffirmed this core belief. I learned not to trust, not to depend on people, and not to believe in relationships whatsoever. The result was a feeling of isolation, a fear of people and, mostly, loneliness.

Thankfully, I was able to realize my actions and behaviors and their consequences. And I was able to change. Slowly, over time, I began to bond with people and see the benefits of leaning on friends to celebrate joy, discuss concerns, and share pain. That is what friends are there to do. Now I have several close friends, and I really do not know where I'd be without them. They accept me just the way I am at all times, even when I feel completely unlovable.

    I have lost many connections over the years due to a lack of time and effort. But I know that it is never too late to rekindle what once was a strong union. Today is the day to reconnect, reestablish the bonds, be a friend to people and let them know how much you truly need their love and care. Friends are true blessings. Friends allow us to explore our personalities without the fear of rejection. Friends let us be ourselves; they let us be free. They are there to gently remind us when we are wrong and to be examples of good people, grounded in truth.

Friendship and the need to get together to talk and to spend time together is invaluable. Friends help us put our, often chaotic, lives into perspective and they offer us unique points of view. Make friendships a priority in your life, nurture them, and cherish their bountiful gifts.

Gratitude

"Gratitude is the most exquisite form of courtesy."

- Jacques Maritain

There is always something for which to be grateful. No matter how tough life gets, no matter how many events fail to go your way, there is an opportunity to be thankful. Gratitude helps us feel full, complete and whole.

As I sit here, I can think of a lot of negative "clutter" that makes me sad, angry, frustrated and depressed. But dwelling on the wrongs is not right. I can also think of things that make me grateful: friends, family, an education, a good job, health and the fact that am alive today. Not everyone is as lucky as I. I must remember how much freedom I have, how many opportunities are afforded me, and how many achievements I have reached. Moreover, I am learning that there is such joy in the little things: a good cup of coffee, a smile, or a reconnection with a friend. There is so much to appreciate in a world of freedom. I think it all comes down to your perspective. Do you choose to view the glass as half full or half empty? It really is your choice: the former being the more obvious and fulfilling choice.

    Gratitude is a special gift because it is the realization and acceptance of what you have, not in a material sense but in a spiritual sense: peace of mind, inner contentment, love and joy - all that make you whole and complete. To be grateful is to be humble. To be grateful is the ability to count your blessings not your sorrows. There is so much for which to be thankful.

Be grateful and have a thankful heart for all that you have been blessed with, and for all the gifts yet to come your way.

Generosity

"Give what you have, give who you are."

- Anonymous

There is, absolutely, joy in giving. Giving brings us a feeling of fullness and expansion and choice; the more we make the choice, the more we experience the feeling. Spontaneous, selfless acts of kindness are simple and effortless, and yet the rewards are so great. Giving brings us pleasure and happiness. Giving can prove to be a limitless treasure that can result in immeasurable delight.

It is good to give. Giving is a great mood elevator. Giving can heal. It is also good for our health. It can even alleviate fear. For personal well-being, giving is amazing medication. Giving involves people and, therefore, it is a fantastic way to establish and maintain connections with people. Bonds formed by acts of kindness and generosity are invaluable. Being generous allows us to uplift and encourage people but, mostly, it is a chance to provide others with hope.

Finally, giving affords us the opportunity to see the truth about life. We can look deeply at ourselves, at nature and at others. There is a sense of unity and oneness that accompanies the spirit of generosity. It is the ultimate form of sharing our most valuable commodity, ourselves.

Generosity is interesting to me because no matter how badly I may feel about myself, I always feel better by offering something I have to somebody else. Whether that offering is knowledge, information, a smile, a hug or a material gift, instantly, I get pleasure and whatever worry I had dissipates. There is definitely something magical about sharing a part of ourselves. I always want to ask myself, "what can I give back?" and "how can I help?" We all have so much to give; it is only a natural extension of ourselves to be generous.

Never believe you have nothing to give. Start by using what you have to bless others. The strong desire to give will allow you to search for ways to do so. In the process of giving, I have learned I do not need to have money to be a blessing to others. Simply caring, listening and being there is plenty. We all need to be edified, complimented and appreciated. We all get weary and need other people. And the more we use our resources to help others, the more we will be blessed. Living to meet the needs of others will bring you great joy and happiness.

Generosity helps us to see there is really no difference between giving and receiving. What you give is what you get.

Reflecting

"When we are no longer able to change a situation, we are challenged to change ourselves."

- Victor Frankl

One of my favorite pastimes is reflecting. I thoroughly enjoy every chance I get to look back on an event or a special day and write about what I think, how I feel, what I would do differently, what I would do the same, how I learned and how I grew. The time I spend reflecting is extremely valuable because it is by reflecting that I am increasing my awareness and understanding. I am learning, and I am continually becoming a better person. Reflecting keeps me focused, balanced and whole. I get a certain serenity and calming feeling from exploring my thoughts and feelings.

    I began formally reflecting about two years ago when I was asked to reflect on a book I had read. Immediately, I was filled with doubts and fears. What should I write? How much should I write? Is what I have good enough? Questions, such as these, flooded my head and, even worse, I received few answers. Why? Because there are no right answers! A reflection is exactly what you want it to be. There are no rules or requirements. How you reflect is your choice from the length to the style to the topic of discussion. Once I embraced this notion of "ultimate creative freedom" and understood my reflections were to be directed by me and exclusive to me, I found a hidden treasure: independence as I had never felt it before.

If you think of your reflection when you look in the mirror, what you see is who you are; but what you see is your view of who you are. It may not be accurate and it may not be what others see. However, it does not matter because it is what you see. The image staring back at you is not right, nor is it wrong; it just is what it is. Therefore, a written reflection is your perception of an event or a thought. It is the truth of the world as seen through your unique eyes.

Reflecting is now an integral part of my life. I use this practice upon the completion of a book, after attending a course, at work and personally. It takes effort and time but I make the time because even ten minutes a day affords me the opportunity to clarify my thoughts and further know and define myself.

Always make time to reflect on your life. Reflecting is a powerful tool that inevitably leads to increased self-awareness, self-understanding and growth.

Pain

"Pain and death are a part of life. To reject them is to reject life itself."
                         - Havelock Ellis

     Today I am an expert of pain. I have just returned from a visit to the dentist. Needless to say, it wasn't pleasurable. If nothing else, this experience did get me thinking deeply about pain and suffering - how much I hate pain, and what measures I take to avoid discomfort of any kind. For the duration of my dentist visit, all I could think about was how much I was looking forward to the time when the pain would subside. I promised myself to really appreciate my life and all of the little things I had previously taken for granted. I could think of nothing else but sipping on a nice hot cup of coffee or slowly and methodically licking an ice cream treat.

Regardless of my over-dramatization of this event, I learned that pain is a clue, a "wake up call", for us to appreciate the good times and cherish the moments. There is physical pain and there is emotional pain. I believe the latter is most often harder to endure. Emotional pain - sadness, rejection, isolation, anger, and depression - is often hidden, repressed or buried pain (even from ourselves). This pain tends to manifest in other forms: getting angry at an innocent loved one, an uncalled for insult, an unexplainable temper tantrum or even the "silent treatment".

Whenever I am in pain, I feel that I gain new perspective. This is because as the pain subsides (and it always does), I feel I am a little more wise, a little more compassionate and a little more empathetic to the needs of others. Additionally, I am always more thankful for my blessings. If these feelings are the price I must pay for pain, I will pay it because it is always a fair tradeoff. There is great satisfaction in overcoming adversity, a real triumph, even if it is simply the dentist!

Nobody likes pain, but pain is unavoidable. And by enduring it, we often learn that life is better than we once believed it to be.

Purpose

"Today a new sun rises for me; everything lives, everything is animated, everything seems to speak to me of my passion, everything invites me to cherish it."
- Anne De Lendos

Purpose gives us direction, keeps us focused and motivates us to move forward. We all have a purpose in life. We are all put on this earth for a specific reason. We all have a job to accomplish. The challenge is to find what that purpose is.

One of the BIG lessons in my life so far has been the realization that I am an important part of this world. I serve a purpose. I am needed by my friends and family. And, yes, I have a mission in life. People need me. People come to me for advice, understanding and care. I watch how they look at me, and I realize how much I am valued.

This was not always the case. I think we all go through times when we have thoughts such as, "why am I here?", "what is my purpose?", "would anyone notice if I wasn't here?" These are tough, yet important questions, and questions that both demand and deserve our attention. By probing into ourselves for the answers, I think the understanding, or our purpose for being here, will become obvious.

What is your purpose? What unique gifts and talents do you bring to your life? What is so special about you? What can you do to leave this world a better place than you found it? What can you offer to those around you?

There is no better feeling in the world than knowing you have a purpose. You are needed in this world, and you are important. You are meant to be here.

About the Author

Lindsay is an educator currently living in Vancouver, British Columbia. She is passionate about running, reading, singing, and writing. Lindsay enjoys spending time with her family and friends. As a lifelong learner, she is committed to personal and professional growth and development, especially is the areas of balance, leadership, and communication. She aspires to obtain a doctoral degree in Education and then teach leadership at the university level. Lindsay is at the beginning of her journey of self-discovery and is eager to share the simple life lessons she has learned so far.

ISBN 1553951174